Botanical Coloring Book for Adults

CARNATION

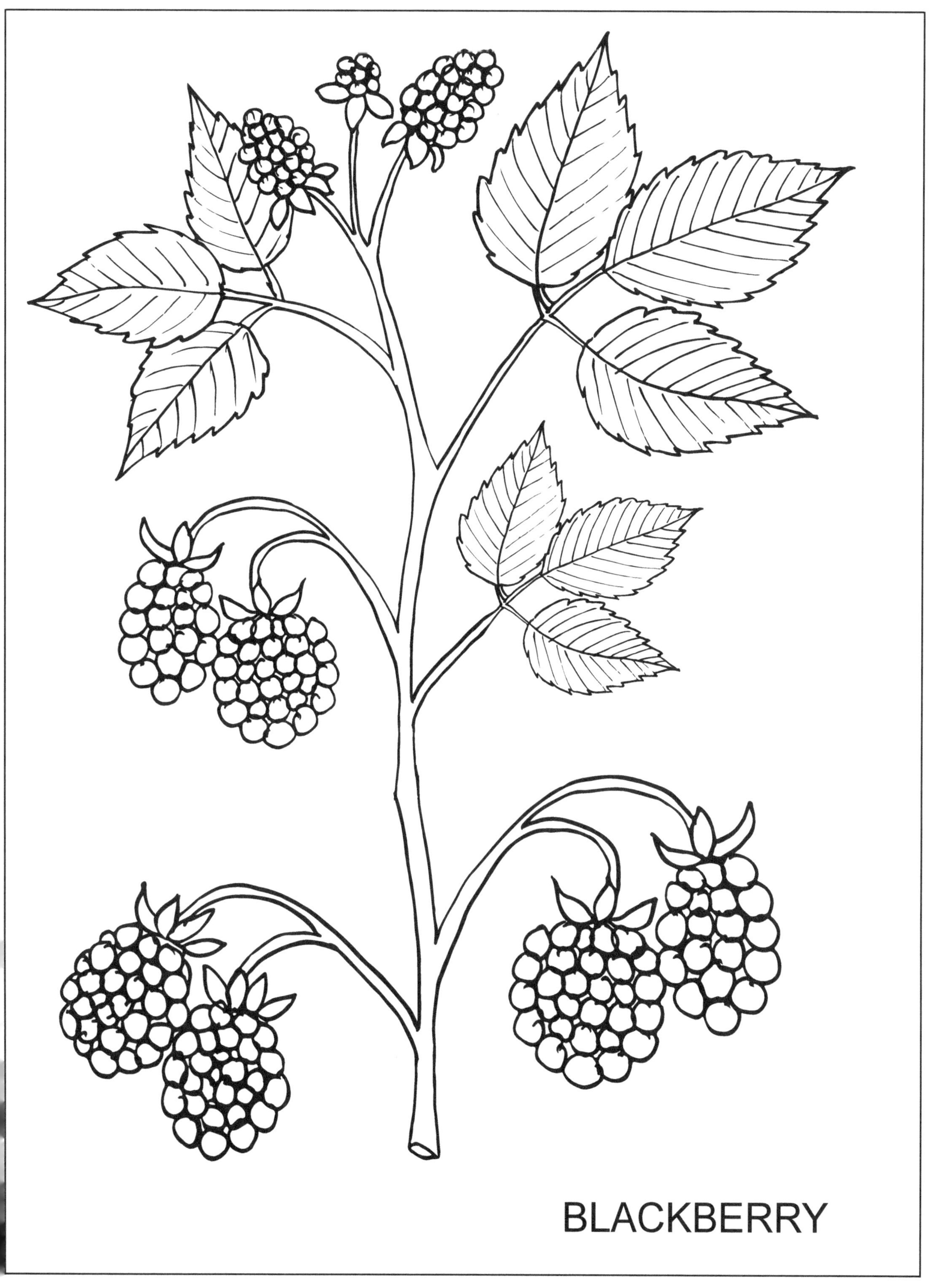

BLACKBERRY

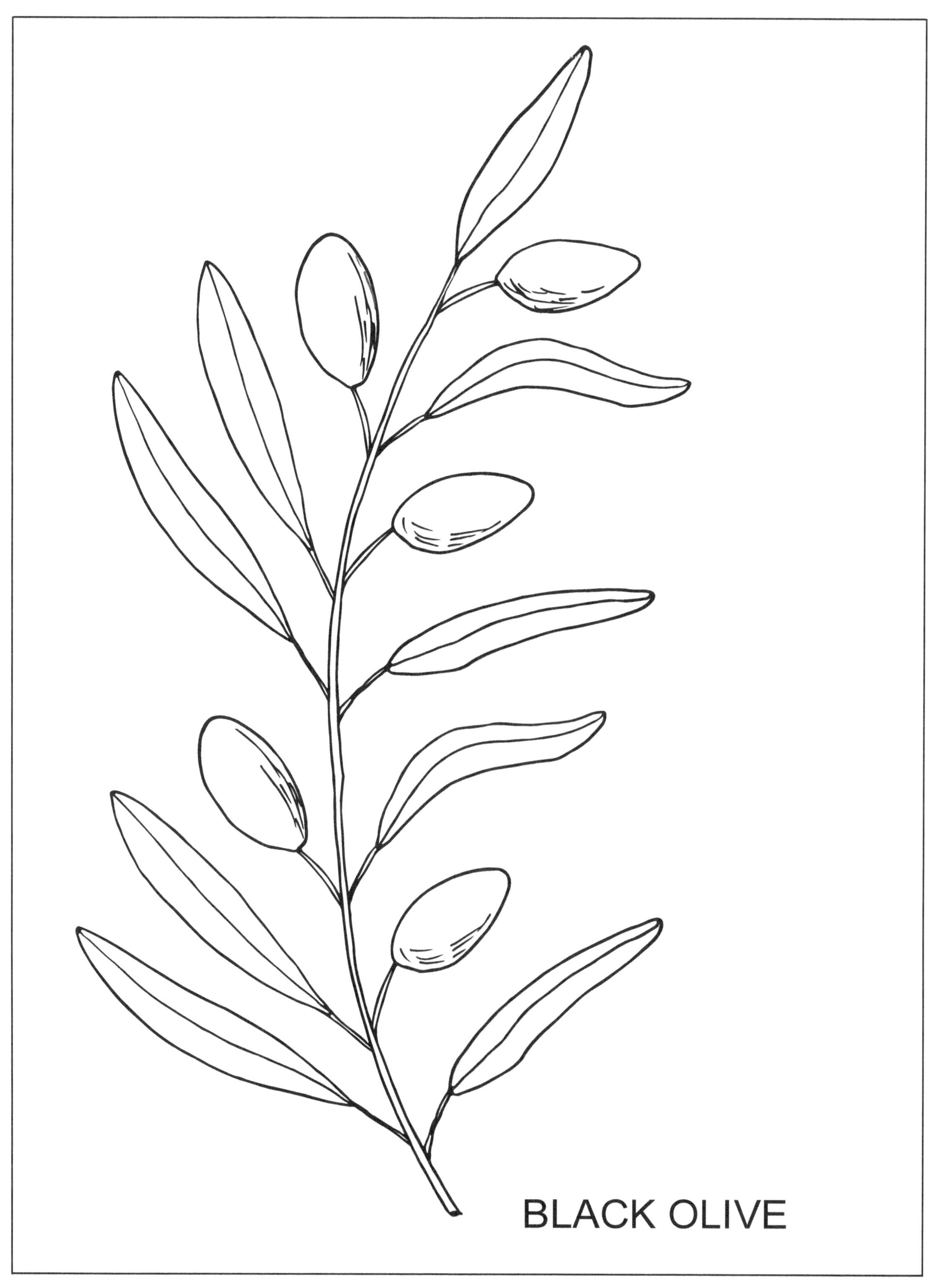

BLACK OLIVE

RASPBERRY

ELDERBERRY

CRANBERRY

CHAMOMILE

PLANTAIN

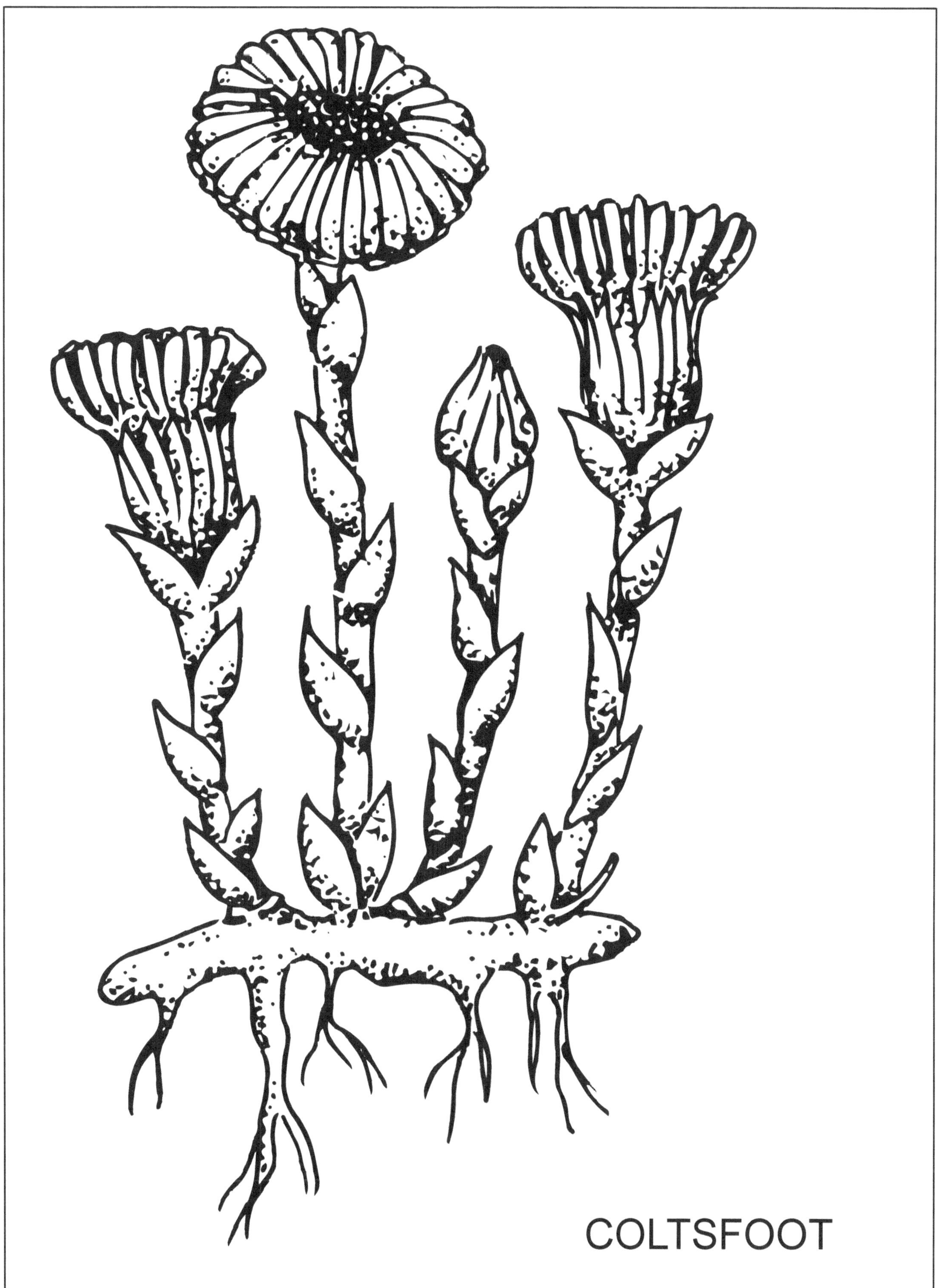

COLTSFOOT

LILY

PEONY

NARCISSUS

CORNFLOWER

CROCUS

VIOLET

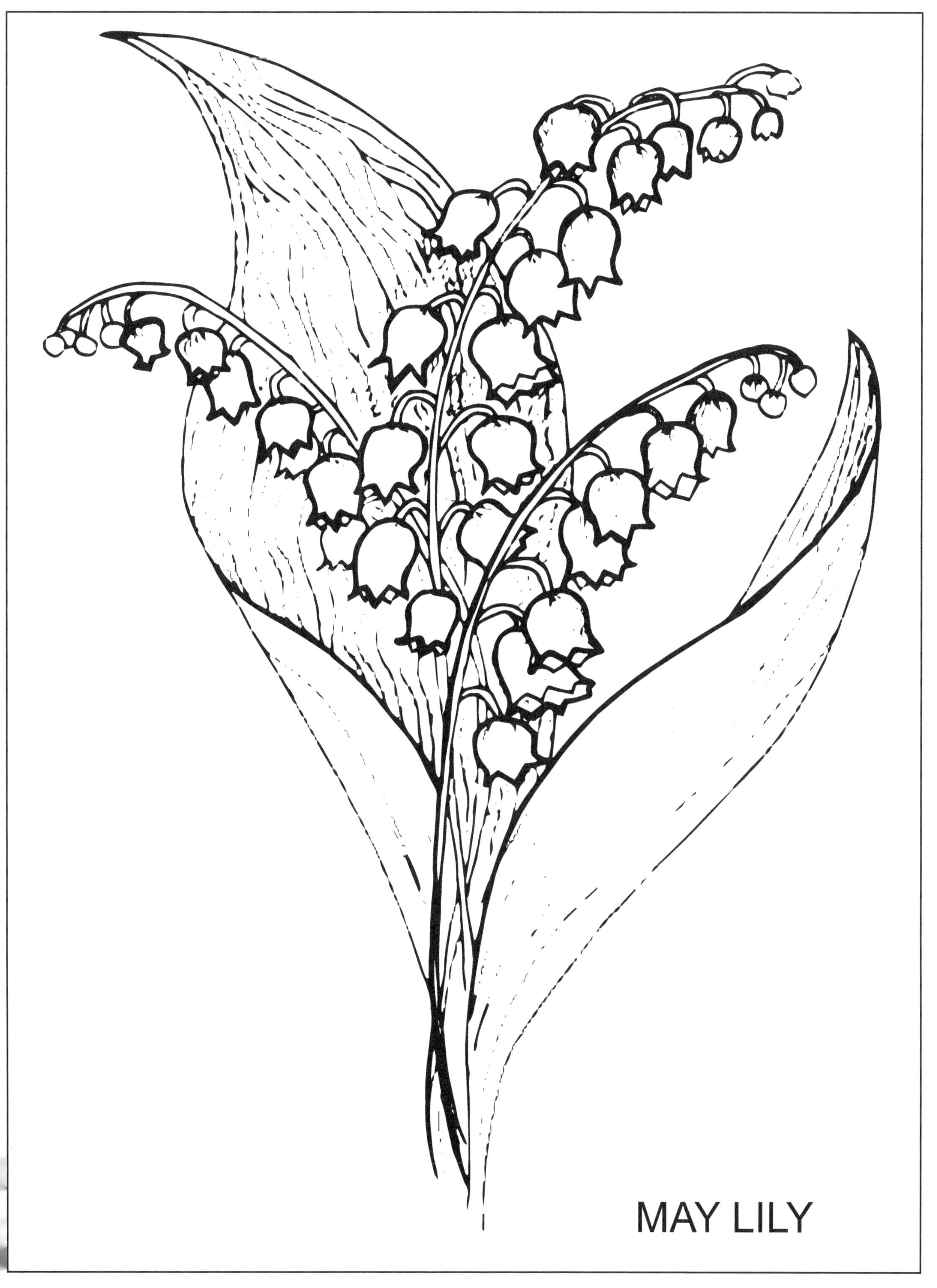

MAY LILY

IRIS

POPPY

JASMINUM

HYACINTH

WILD ROSEMARY

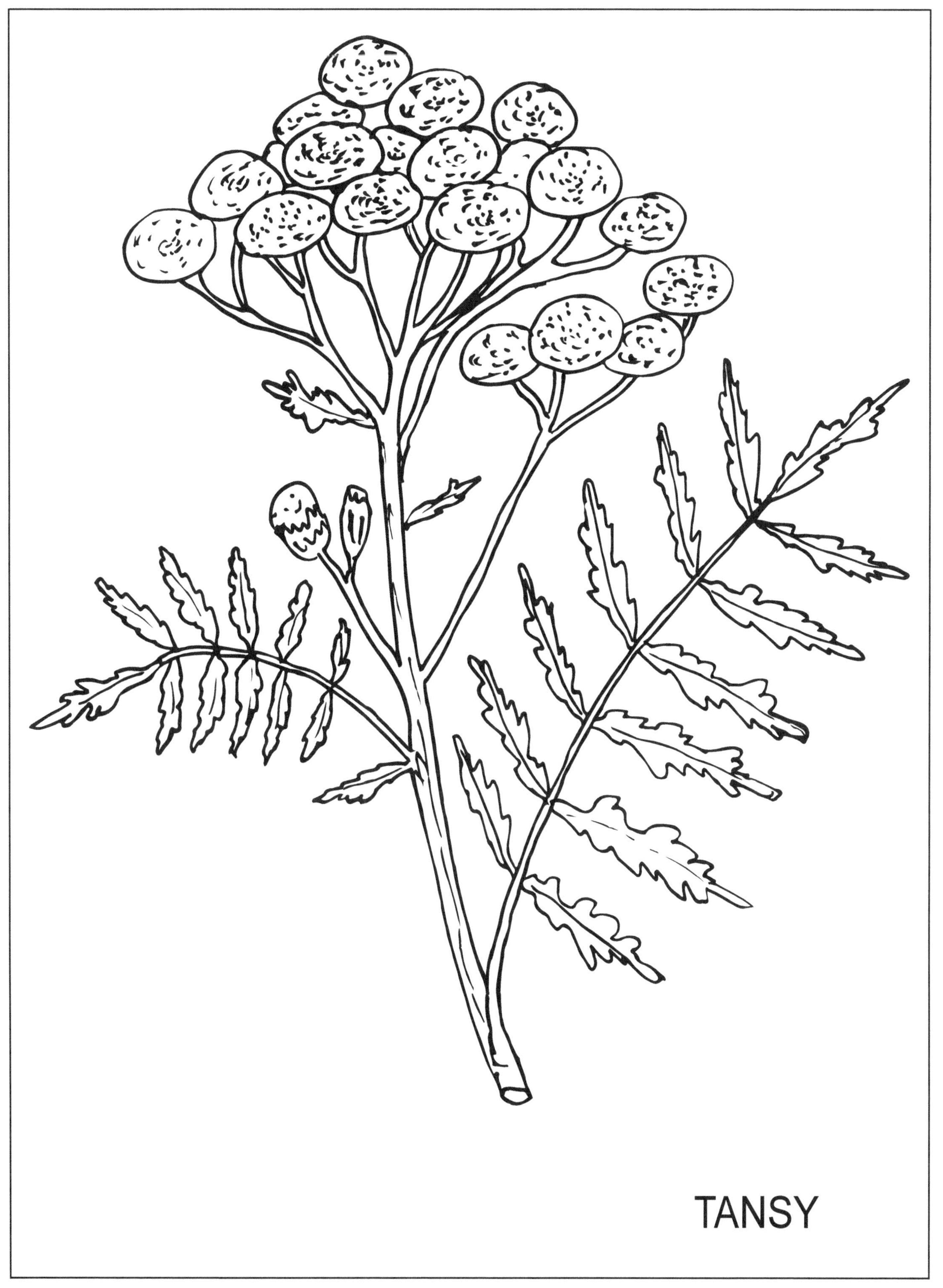

TANSY

FIREWEED

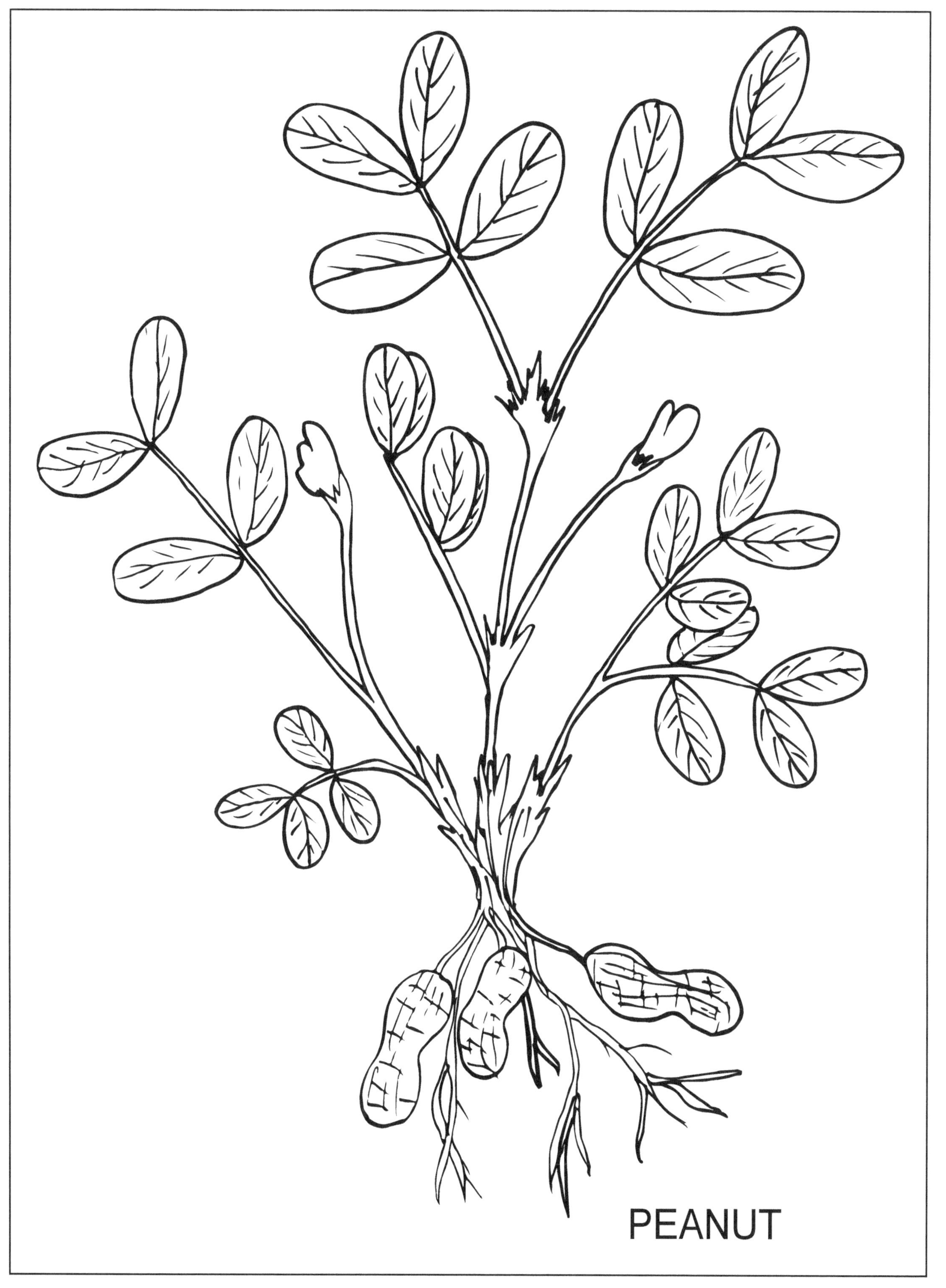

PEANUT

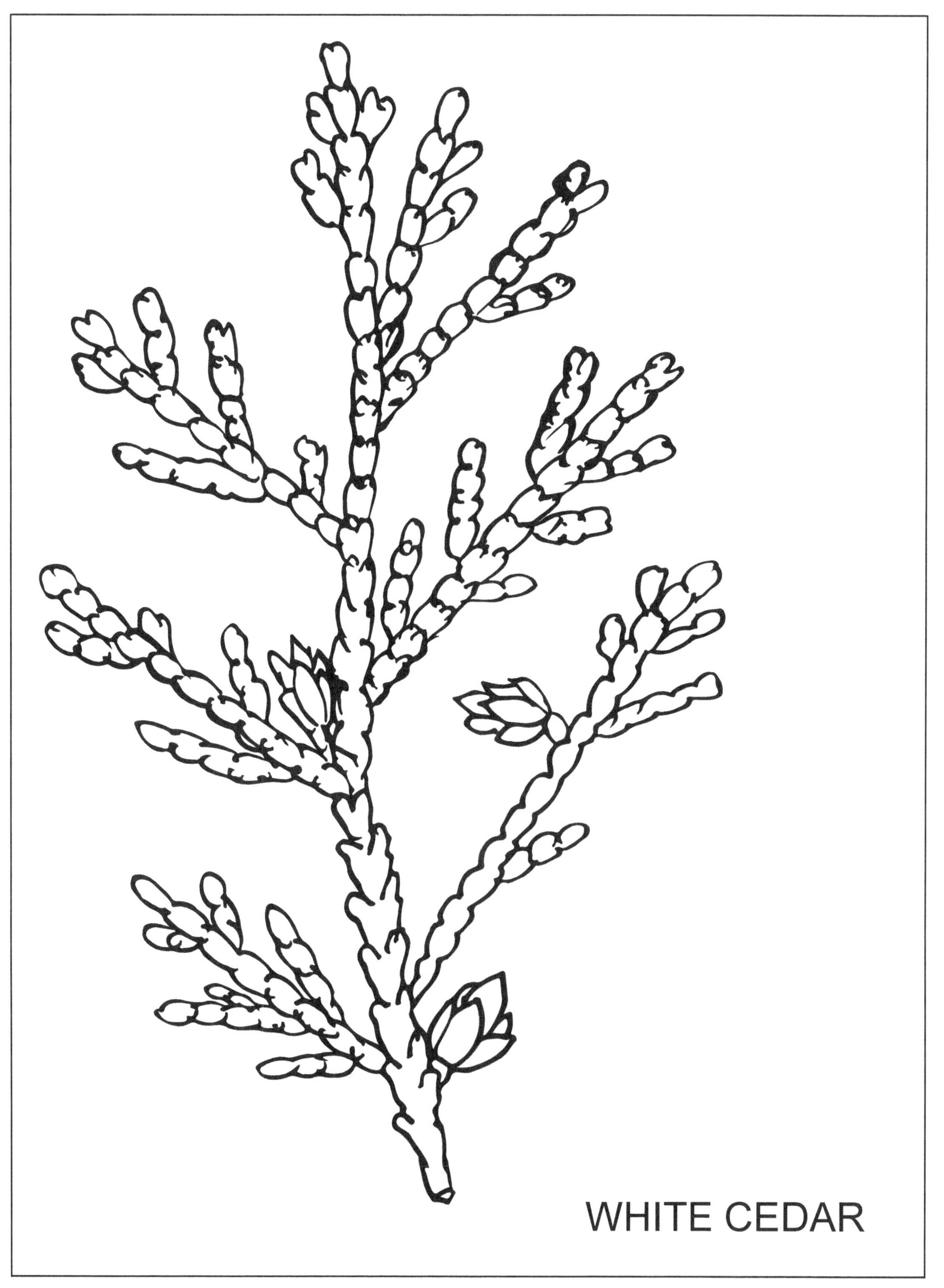

WHITE CEDAR

JIMSON WEED

HYPERICUM

VALERIAN

SALVIA

CALENDULA

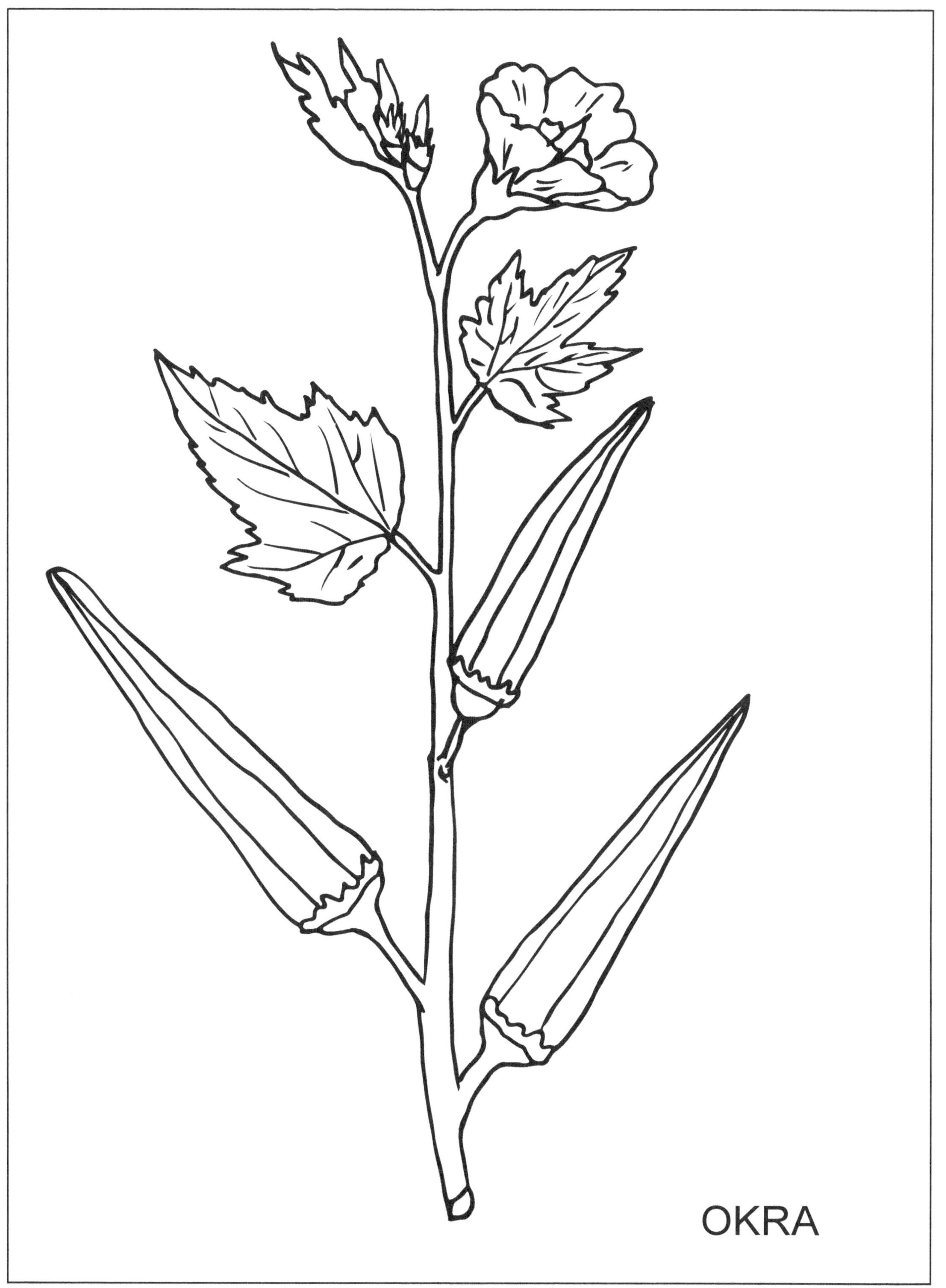

OKRA

IVY

TEA TREE

BOG - MYRTLE

BUGLEHERB

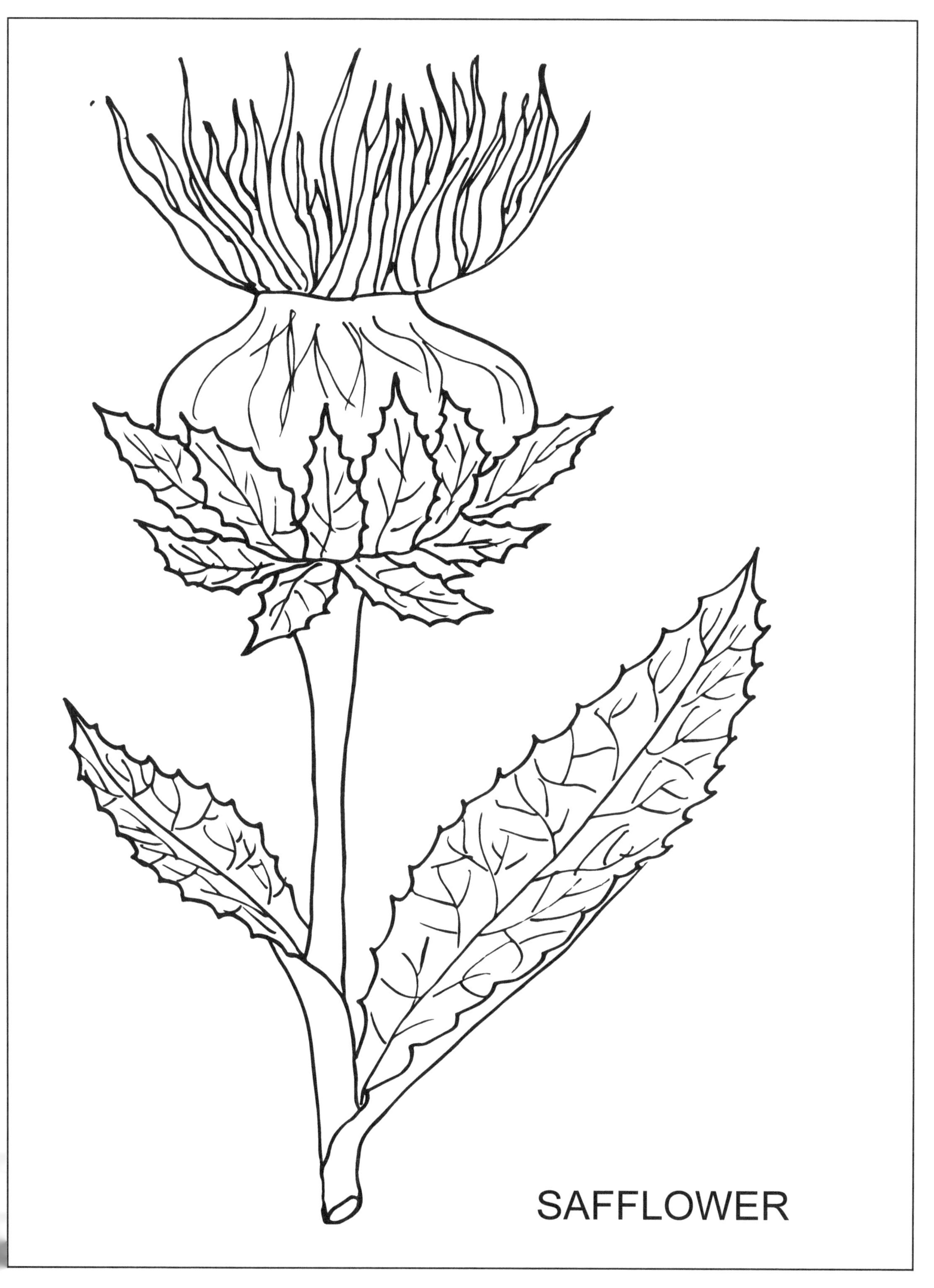

SAFFLOWER

BUTTERFLY PEA FLOWER

LICORICE

JIAOGULAN

BUTTERBUR

INDIAN TOBACCO

CHICK WEED

YELLOW DOCK

FIGWORT

ANISE

CAMPHOR

CLEMATIS

JASMINE FLOWER

BALLOON FLOWER

VANILLA

Here's a special gift from ColoKara for purchasing this coloring book!

You can now freely download these coloring pages at any time and print them out as many times as you want!

Get your FREE coloring pages from this link: https://colokara.com/botanical-coloring-green

HAPPY COLORING!

Credit Images to - Zabavina, Foxyliam, Sudarat Wilairat, Vera Petruk, Tashadraw, Mamita